God's Little Instruction Book

Honor Books
Tulsa, Oklahoma

God's Little Instruction Book, mini edition
ISBN 1-56292-764-7
Copyright © 1999 by Honor Books
P.O. Box 55388
Tulsa, Oklahoma 74155

Manuscript compiled by W. B. Freeman Concepts, Inc.,
Tulsa, Oklahoma

All quotations without attributions are considered to be anonymous.

References

Unless otherwise indicated, all Scripture quotations are taken from the *King James Version* of the Bible.

Scripture quotations marked NIV are taken from the *Holy Bible, New International Version* ®. NIV ®. Copyright © 1973, 1978, 1984 by International Bible Society. Used by permission of Zondervan Publishing House. All rights reserved.

Scripture quotations marked NASB are taken from the *New American Standard Bible*. Copyright © The Lockman Foundation 1960, 1962, 1963, 1968, 1971, 1972, 1973, 1975, 1977. Used by permission.

Introduction

In this new mini-edition of the best-selling *God's Little Instruction Book*, we've again paired your favorite inspirational quotations with God's amazing Scriptures, then illustrated it with a visual feast of four-color art and photos depicting this incredibly beautiful world in which we live.

This tiny little book is the perfect size to pop into your purse for a refreshing break during your busy day, or give as an inexpensive gift to a friend or family member. Share the gift of God's love with others!

Return to its refreshing pages time and again when you need renewed vision and direction. Let God inspire you to reach your full potential! Then watch your dreams come true as you put His wisdom to work in your life.

*Real friends are those who,
when you've made a fool of
yourself, don't feel you've
done a permanent job.*

— Erwin T. Randall

[Charity] beareth all things,
believeth all things, hopeth
all things, endureth all things.
Charity never faileth.

❦ 1 Corinthians 13:7-8 ❦

*Patience is the ability
to keep your motor idling
when you feel like
stripping your gears.*

He that is slow to anger is better
than the mighty; and he that ruleth
his spirit than he that taketh a city.

❧ Proverbs 16:32 ❧

Remember the banana—
when it left the bunch,
it got skinned.

Not forsaking the assembling
of ourselves together, as the manner
of some is; but exhorting one
another: and so much the more,
as ye see the day approaching.

❧ Hebrews 10:25 ❧

Many a good man has failed because he had his wishbone where his backbone should have been.

Be strong and of a good courage; be not afraid, neither be thou dismayed: for the LORD thy God is with thee whithersoever thou goest.

❧ Joshua 1:9 ❧

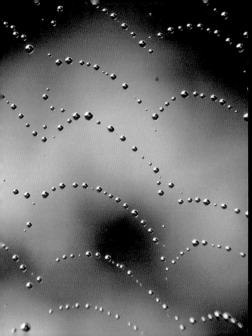

*If at first you don't
succeed, try reading
the instructions.*

Take fast hold of instruction; let her
not go: keep her; for she is thy life.

❧ Proverbs 4:13 ❧

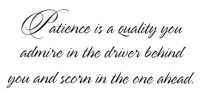

Patience is a quality you admire in the driver behind you and scorn in the one ahead.

Patience is better than pride. Do not be quickly provoked in your spirit, for anger resides in the lap of fools.

❧ Ecclesiastes 7:8-9 NIV ❧

Some people complain because God put thorns on roses, while others praise Him for putting roses among thorns.

Finally, brethern, whatsoever things are true, whatsoever things are honest, whatsoever things are just, whatsoever things are pure, whatsoever things are lovely, whatsoever things are of good report; if there be any virtue, and if there be any praise, think on these things.

❧ Philippians 4:8 ❧

CRIMSON RO

The bridge you burn
now may be the one you
later have to cross.

If it be possible, as much as lieth in you, live peaceably with all men.

❧ Romans 12:18 ❧

*The measure of a man
is not how great his faith is,
but how great his love is.*

–J. C. Watts

And now these three remain:
faith, hope and love. But the
greatest of these is love.

🕊 1 Corinthians 13:13 NIV 🕊

The grass may look greener on the other side, but it still has to be mowed.

—Little Richard

Be content with such
things as ye have.

❧ Hebrews 13:5 ❧

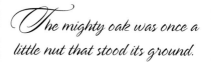

The mighty oak was once a little nut that stood its ground.

A man shall not be established
by wickedness: but the root of
the righteous shall not be moved.

❧ Proverbs 12:3 ❧

Most people wish to serve God—but only in an advisory capacity.

—Rev. Gary McIntosh

Humble yourselves therefore under the mighty hand of God, that he may exalt you in due time.

🕊 1 Peter 5:6 🕊

*Most men forget God
all day and ask Him to
remember them at night.*

Evening, and morning, and at noon,
will I pray, and cry aloud:
and he shall hear my voice.

❧ Psalm 55:17 ❧

You should never let adversity get you down— except on your knees.

Is any one of you in trouble?
He should pray.

❧ James 5:13 NIV ❧

It's good to be a Christian and know it, but it's better to be a Christian and show it!

By this shall all men know that ye are my disciples, if ye have love one to another.

❧ John 13:35 ❧

Sorrow looks back.

Worry looks around.

Faith looks up.

Fixing our eyes on Jesus, the author and perfecter of faith, who for the joy set before Him endured the cross, despising the shame, and has sat down at the right hand of the throne of God.

❧ Hebrews 12:2 NASB ❧

A man is never in worse company than when he flies into a rage and is beside himself.

–Jacob M. Braude

He that is soon angry
dealeth foolishly.

❧ Proverbs 14:17 ❧

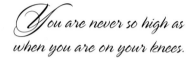

You are never so high as when you are on your knees.

—Jean Hodges

Humble yourselves in the sight of the Lord, and he shall lift you up.

🦋 James 4:10 🦋

The secret of contentment is the realization that life is a gift, not a right.

But godliness with contentment is great gain.

❧ 1 Timothy 6:6 ❧

Falling down doesn't make you a failure, but staying down does.

For a just man falleth seven times,
and riseth up again.

❧ Proverbs 24:16 ❧

*Time is more valuable
than money because time
is irreplaceable.*

Redeeming the time, because
the days are evil.

❦ Ephesians 5:16 ❦

God can heal a broken heart, but He has to have all the pieces.

My son, give me thine heart.

❧ Proverbs 23:26 ❧

*Authority makes
some people grow and
others just swell.*

But he that is greatest among
you shall be your servant.

❧ Matthew 23:11 ❧

*Be more concerned
with what God thinks
about you than what
people think about you.*

Then Peter and the other apostles
answered and said, We ought to
obey God rather than men.

❧ Acts 5:29 ❧

When confronted with a Goliath-sized problem, which way do you respond: "He's too big to hit," or like David, "He's too big to miss"?

The LORD that delivered me out of the paw of the lion, and out of the paw of the bear, he will deliver me out of the hand of this Philistine.

❧ 1 Samuel 17:37 ❧

*Forget yourself for others,
and others will not forget you!*

— John Bauer

Therefore all things whatsoever ye
would that men should do to you,
do ye even so to them: for this is
the law and the prophets.

❧ Matthew 7:12 ❧

*Those who bring sunshine
into the lives of others cannot
keep it from themselves.*

—Sir James Matthew Barrie

Be not deceived; God is not mocked:
for whatsoever a man soweth,
that shall he also reap.

🌿 Galatians 6:7 🌿

No man ever really finds out what he believes in until he begins to instruct his children.

And, ye fathers, provoke not your children to wrath: but bring them up in the nurture and admonition of the Lord.

❧ Ephesians 6:4 ❧

*Contentment isn't getting
what we want but being
satisfied with what we have.*

Not that I speak in respect of want:
for I have learned, in whatsoever
state I am, therewith to be content.

❧ Philippians 4:11 ❧

Ability will enable a man to go to the top, but it takes character to keep him there.

– Mike Murdock

The righteousness of the blameless
makes a straight way for them,
but the wicked are brought down
by their own wickedness.

❧ Proverbs 11:5 NIV ❧

*Your words are windows
to your heart.*

For out of the abundance of the
heart the mouth speaketh.

❧ Matthew 12:34 ❧

A shut mouth gathers no foot.

He that keepeth his mouth keepeth his life: but he that openeth wide his lips shall have destruction.

❧ Proverbs 13:3 ❧

Do the thing you fear,
and the death of fear

is certain.

—*Ralph Waldo Emerson*

Be strong and of a good courage,
fear not, nor be afraid of them:
for the LORD thy God, he it is
that doth go with thee; he will
not fail thee, nor forsake thee.

❧ Deuteronomy 31:6 ❧

God plus one
is always a majority!

—Doug Wead

If God be for us,
who can be against us?

❧ Romans 8:31 ❧

Whoever gossips to you

will be a gossip of you.

—Spanish Proverb

A talebearer revealeth secrets:
but he that is of a faithful spirit
concealeth the matter.

❦ Proverbs 11:13 ❦

Every person should have a special cemetery plot in which to bury the faults of friends and loved ones.

—Ralph Waldo Emerson

And be ye kind one to another,
tenderhearted, forgiving one another,
even as God for Christ's sake
hath forgiven you.

❧ Ephesians 4:32 ❧

The greatest possession you have is the twenty-four hours directly in front of you.

–Doug Wead

For there is a time there for every purpose and for every work.

❧ Ecclesiastes 3:17 ❧

The most valuable gift
you can give another is
a good example.

—Spanish Proverb

For I have given you an example, that
ye should do as I have done to you.

❧ John 13:15 ❧

If you feel "dog tired" at night, maybe it's because you "growled" all day.

If it be possible, as much as lieth in you, live peaceably with all men.

❧ Romans 12:18 ❧

He who cannot forgive
breaks the bridge over
which he himself must pass.

–George Herbert

For if ye forgive men their trespasses,
your heavenly Father will
also forgive you.

❦ Matthew 6:14 ❦

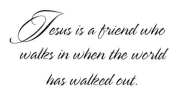

Jesus is a friend who walks in when the world has walked out.

These things I have spoken unto you, that in me ye might have peace. In the world ye shall have tribulation: but be of good cheer; I have overcome the world.

❧ John 16:33 ❧

Faith is daring the soul to go beyond what the eyes can see.

– J. R. R. Tolkien

For we walk by faith, not by sight.

❧ 2 Corinthians 5:7 ❧

88

The person who does things that count doesn't usually stop to count them.

One thing I do: Forgetting what is behind and straining toward what is ahead, I press on toward the goal.

❧ Philippians 3:13-14 NIV ❧

You can accomplish more in one hour with God than in one lifetime without Him.

With God all things are possible.

❧ Matthew 19:26 ❧

*Humor is to life
what shock absorbers
are to automobiles.*

–Sister Mary Christelle Macaluso

A merry heart doeth good
like a medicine: but a broken
spirit drieth the bones.

❧ Proverbs 17:22 ❧

If you have enjoyed this book, or
if it has impacted your life, we
would like to hear from you.
Please contact us at:

Honor Books
Department E
P.O. Box 55388
Tulsa, Oklahoma 74155
Or by e-mail at: info@honorbooks.com

Additional copies of this book and other
titles in the *God's Little Instruction Book* series
are available from your
local bookstore.

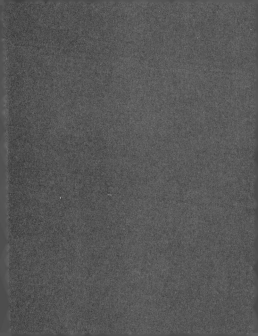

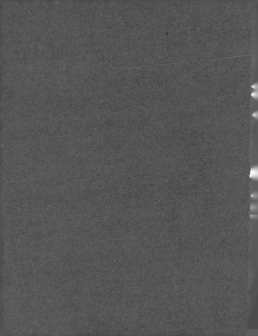